Satin Preludes

Indra Watson

BookLeaf
Publishing

India | USA | UK

Presentation by *BookLeaf Publishing*

Web: www.bookleafpub.com

E-mail: info@bookleafpub.com

ISBN: 9789357214728

First edition 2022

PREFACE

If you've ever wore or seen a satin dress on someone, one of the first things you may notice is how transparent and clingy it can be. Satin clothing, depending on the style may or may not be flattering or unforgiving. However, the satin weave has an elegance that cannot be ignored, protects moisture when used as a pillowcase, and can withstand situations that would make most other types of clothing wrinkle. It is durable but even the slightest mistake in it's make can be noticeable.

I say all this to preface the origin for the title of this book. As my second published collection of poetry, I wanted to take an authentic approach at some of the more interpersonal experiences I have had in my life. Satin Preludes is meant to be a couple chapters short of an artistic attempt to provide a prelude to my human and spiritual struggles. This prelude is meant to weave together fragments of my life into an eloquent yet truthful garment.

It may not be a one-size-fits-all piece but it is my sincere hope that something within these covers and between these sheets of paper help

you find that sense of knowing that you aren't
alone.

Empathic Epitome of Eros Love

There are so many I did love.
In the end they couldn't return the sentiment like
the One above.

Searching for something only God can give me.
Pouring out my cup to loveless lovers has left
me empty.

The Lord shed His light in the crevices of my
insecurities.
He has brought me redemption from all of my
impurities.

No Home for my Head

For months I slept in my car every night.
Waking up for work with the daylight.

Shower at the gym and change into clothes from
my storage unit that are clean.
Head to the laundromat in the evening and pray I
can afford a can of beans.

I knew God was always carrying me.
Every day in that dark tunnel that made it hard
to see.

I praised Him for a roof over my head.
I praised Him for every time I was fed.

I praised Him for the cloth of my backseat to
rest my head.
I never stopped praising Him through each tear I
shed.

For I knew these moments were making me
humble.
I knew these dark times were strengthening me
for the next stumble.

There were times I choked on my pride.
There's nothing you can't get through with Jesus
by your side.

That's all you really need to persevere.
To feel His presence and know He is near.

Accepting help was one of the hardest things to
do.
But God opens doors and works through people
too.

Bitsy Bipolar

Bipolar is like a beast inside my mind that wants
to breed.
It has an insatiable appetite I try not to feed.

This balancing act has me exhausted.
I was in a happy mood earlier and then I lost it.

I pray I am emotionally equipped to accept this
challenge.
'Cause there's no telling when my chemicals will
get imbalanced.

I'm walking a proverbial tight rope.
I fall down but don't lose hope.

Pawned Petals

He said he'd make a woman out of me.
So I tasted the forbidden fruit at 23.
It wasn't the romantic event I expected.
Things went farther than I intended.
I drove away with my innocence behind me.
Somehow I thought I'd feel more free.
I started to feel less empowered.
A black rose deflowered.
He loves me, he loves me not.
Upon his mattress lies a blood spot.
A reminder that I was once beguiled.
Remnants of a girl defiled.
The guilt crept on me almost everyday.
I just couldn't stay away.
Over the hills and through the valley,
I would travel for him to see me.
I prayed for forgiveness to God above.
I was desperate to call this love.
I was longing for a relationship status.
There was never going to be an us.
A few months shy of 4 years I walked away.
It was time to do things God's way.

Leave That Lane

Love in the fast lane leads to so much pain.
But linear loneliness can drive you insane.
There is Someone who wants to wrap you in
Their arms tight.
You can talk all day, not just when you pray at
night.
He came down on earth in human form.
You can trust Him to keep you safe in the eye of
life's storm.

Crossing Rainbows for you

I'm fighting demons in my mind.
They're making me break stride.
Towards everything I thought was missing.
I can forget that when we're kissing.

I am staying out of touch.
With people that I trust.
I feel like my heart could sink.
Deeper than an iceberg on the brink.

Someone give me water.
I can barely speak or utter.
My emotions are dry and old.
Like this frog inside my throat.

It's waiting to escape with words I once clung to.
I hang onto everything you say when aloof.
You stay silent lately.
How could I not see you berate me?

Delusions tell me I'm in love with you.
I want to wait this out but patience is
disillusioned too.
It might break inside me and sever a heartstring.
These emotions are so inviting.

What if it starts to bleed?
Will I finally then be there for me?
I'm forgetting how to remember how to love
myself.
I analyze between the lines I've drawn myself.

'Cause all your words appear to be a cryptic
disguise.
I welcome another hello to your every goodbye.
Why can't you mean what you say?
Is it too hard to be taken literally?

I keep giving myself away.
Hoping you'll love me back one day.
But friends is all we're staying.
Is it a game that we're playing?

It's fun when we are just laying there looking at
a star.
Gentle reminders of a friendship gone too far.
Eventually all the constellations go to sleep.
That's when we hideaway from being "we."

You put hope on a shelf that can't be reached.
My emotional intelligence is vertically
challenged.
I can slow down if you want me to.
But I can't stop again for you.

This race was always meant to have just one
winner.
Silly of me to think we'd cross finish together.
I keep holding on like you can't stand alone.
I'm finding contentment in the friend zone.

Somehow the depression is comforting.
What kind of cycle have I gotten in?
My pain's no longer a travesty.
He's my definition of majesty.

"Let go and let God" is easier said but will be
done.
If this time is a game, I believe you've won.
Just a rainbow of emotions and you always go
for the pot of gold.
I let you reach the end like it's easy to let go.

Emotionally Emote

I struggle to love me.
Yet I love you effortlessly.

I had to lose us to find me.
Friends is all we'll ever be.

I look for blessings that are disguised.
All the while my worth is compromised.

I'm tirelessly trying to fill this void.
Only God can bring me true joy.

Alcoholism is not Anonymous

Why didn't anyone warn me?
Loving an alcoholic is far from easy.
Some days you tell yourself it's no big deal.
Other times events seem so surreal.
Waiting for your cell to make a familiar sound.
Just to realize they're nowhere to be found.

Maybe I will leave tomorrow.
Maybe I'll run out of sorrow.
Then I'll be numb.
Then I'll be done.
They can't leave you because you're leaving them.
Until you find reasons to stay again.

Hurtful words begin to be exchanged.
How much more can your life be arranged?
They're beginning to appear as a hamster in a wheel.
When we fell in love, was this always part of the deal?
Their breath smells like last night's regret.
Maybe we won't fight if I pretend to forget.

You inch your way closer to them for affection.
Then they reach for the bottle and give you
rejection.
You buy them one more fix because after that
they will give it up.
I think we're both addicted because I can't seem
to be fed up.
One more day in the event that something good
could happen.
Victim of so much abuse my walls are caving in.

I talk to friends just to be called an enabler and
shun.
Congrats alcohol, another battle you have won.
He wants to hold the bottle more than me.
He's succumbing to his disease.
He wants to taste the liquor just because.
I'm forced to question if this is love.

Beneath this multi-faceted illness is a caring
person drowning in booze.
It's that person I hold onto and don't want to
lose.
How is it I have mustered tears yet again?
What do you do when alcohol steals your best
friend?
When the raging starts, I take a deep breath.
If I really leave they'll have nothing left.

I love so hard I've lost my identity.
How could they love aluminum more than me?
There are times they get vulnerable and tap into
my empathy.
Some days they are so close to breaking free.
Just one day if they could be sober.
I pray this nightmare will soon be over.

They're hiding cans, I can hear them rattle.
I've perfected the art of picking and choosing my
battle.
Have they given up on me?
Were we just not meant to be?
My heart is stretched so thin.
I strain to grow thicker skin.

Our family deserves better than this.
I can taste the hops on their lips.
I pray so hard it seems my knees are
disintegrating.
Alcoholism haunted their family for generations.
How do I break this generational sin and curse?
If we try therapy, will things get worse?

I am strong but not invincible.
I feel I am bearing my own crucible.
Would they notice if I walk away?
I'll find out possibly another day.
I can't leave who I love the most.
Even if to them I'm just a codependent ghost.

Gains and Gratefulnes

I praise You in life's sunshine.
I praise You in life's pain.
I praise You when the smiles don't come.
I praise You in the rain.

I praise You in the daylight.
I praise You underneath night skies.
I praise You when the chips are down.
I praise You when the stakes are high.

I praise God for ways He got me through.
For so many things I give God praise.
I praise God for the bad things too.
I want to thank Him all of my days.

Adversities and Adversary

I'm no stranger to adversity.
For I know there's traps from the Adversary.
These trials don't mean God has forsaken me.
I know that He still loves me.
There are times my faith gets put to the test.
In His arms I find rest.

Overture of Ovaries

Polycystic Ovary Syndrome came to me at 17.
She made a home inside of me.
Raging hormones and exuberant mood swings.
Why didn't my medical team warn me of these
things?
They mentioned facial hair and irregular
menstruation.
But the rest of the symptoms they failed to
mention.
Sometimes the pain feels like I'm outside my
body looking in.
Sometimes I wonder why my ovaries are
broken.
There's not much comparable to having a cyst
burst.
I'm thankful for the people who have loved me
through my worst.
My devastation is on the mend.
This syndrome has become my friend.

Bows of Brokenness

Break me a million times if that is what it will
take.
Mold me into what You would like to make.
Pierce my heart a million times if that is what is
necessary.
Help me get dressed in the Armor of God to
battle the Adversary.
Convict me a million times if that will help me
walk the straight and narrow.
I choose to trust the One whose eyes is on the
sparrow.
Hit me with the truth a million times lest I
forget.
I need You most when my will is feeling bent.

The Heaviness of Thinking

I was never one to be led astray.
Then again, I've never felt this way.

There was something about his undeniable
charm.
In my eyes he couldn't do no harm.

His eyes took me to another place.
Then he broke my heart without a trace.

The Art of Not Keeping Him

He couldn't be my man.
But he could hold my hand.

He couldn't let someone get close enough to
break his heart.
Meanwhile that ripped mine apart.

He said he was staying alive for me.
The possessiveness for each other made it hard
for us to breath.

He called me his best friend.
I didn't want those times to end.

But here we are in separation.
This pain seems to be never-ending.

The Scene that I can't Unsee

Hand over throat.
Slow choke.
Losing air and can't speak.
He's toppling over me.
Asking what the text says.
My mind prepares for final rest.
Then he lets go.
I could now answer the question he wanted to know.
But he was ready for something else by then.
I can't get up so my body gives in.
Quiet pleas to stop.
I can't get him off the top.
Reach for my phone but no battery power.
My memory reflects this night as my darkest hour.
Middle of the night he said we needed to have a conversation.
I arrived at his hotel room despite my intuition.
A single tear fell down my cheek.
My inner voice becoming meek.
My conscience scolds for not listening better to my dad and mom.
My friends were in the car waiting for me, not knowing what's wrong.

I pull up my pants and gathered my shame from
an event so vile.
Return to the car and force a smile.
Accepting it happened became harder than what
transpired.
How could I be wronged by a man I admired?
I continued to date him and cowered from
reporting.
Post-traumatic stress disorder aids me in
memory sorting.
I forgave you so that I can forgive me.
My lack of courage is haunting.

Prayer of Peace and Pleas

Holy Spirit fill this place.
Jesus, help me seek Your face.

I want to connect to the Vine again.
This isn't the condition You want me living in.

Holy Spirit help me discern.
Jesus, You are my main concern.

I want to tarry with You throughout each day.
Lord, I don't want nothing outside of Your way.

Help me feel Your mercy all my days.
Your grace motivates me in so many ways.

Please protect me and give me a new song.
I want to praise You all day long.

Best Friends and Best Feelings

His love was pure.
But I was looking for something more.
We had a connection that could endure.
Isn't that what best friends are for?

It took losing him to find the truth within.
I'm out of words to say.
Can we begin again?
My broken heart's in disarray.

We met when I was approximately five.
Then we reunited at a house party.
Being friends as adults made me feel alive.
The rest of him and I is history.

I can tell the story 'til I'm blue in the face.
Next to no one understands.
Our memories my mind cannot erase.
Especially when I listen to our favorite bands.

How can you lose someone you never had?
It's simpler than everyone thinks.
It's not a breakup but hurts just as bad.
Especially when I have our favorite drinks.

A part of me is missing across the county line.
My head is yearning for that familiar place to
rest.
I try to just leave the past love behind.
His absence put my heart to the test.

I'm never lonely.
I am just lost.
The butterflies he gives me keeps me company.
Just to cross paths again, I'd pay 'most any cost.

Maybe this friendship was meant for a season.
Maybe we created too much toxicity.
I just hope love was part of the reason.
Do you still think of me?

Was I not enough or too much?
These feelings were unintentional.
Do you miss my touch?
My love for you is unconditional.

Don't look back, you deserve real peace.
This isn't about us giving up, it's 'bout you not
giving in.
You were the best part of me.
The love you showed outwardly I will store
within.

You're going to make it, I swear.
You showed me true friends and love exist.
I feel closer with every article of your clothing I
wear.
There's a price to pay for passion you can't
resist.

Just friends or modern romance?
A type of feeling that can't be manipulated.
I never stood a chance.
But I stand vindicated.

Analyzing and Auditing the Auditory Thoughts

So many things in the air.
I hear silence everywhere.

There's so much to be said about what's been
broken.
I've found solace in words unspoken.

I've forced myself to feel fine.
I seek the silver line.

Of a cloud I'll never land on.
In this storm you are the sun.

If there is hope I've found some.
I've heard the thunder and expect the lightening
to come.

There are no words for body language you show
me.
Your heartbeat is poetry.

Read me something, like your mind.
I want to hear what you decide.

Immerse me in a sea of your emotion.
My best quality is showing appreciation.

I hope you feel my adoration.
It's hard to regain my patience.

Specifically when your attention is all I'm
yearning.
Losing in love has made me faster at learning.

We Weren't Good at House

You said you wanted to be my spouse.
In the end you just wanted to play house.
All the while the letters expressed love for me.
How foolish to not see your deceit.
Was I a cover-up for a truth you wished to
conceal?
Was there any part of your words that were real?
You gave me your grandmother's necklace,
saying I was special.
Looking back, we didn't have romantic potential.
You said you wanted a family with me.
However, only if the doctor could artificially
inseminate me.
When the lease ended, we did too.
Sometimes loving from a distance is all you can
do.

Searchlight

Searching for a place that feels like home.
My heart is the loneliest place I've ever known.
It's never settled.
There's times it's nestled.
It breaks too easily.
It wants to control me.
I must keep a contrite heart.
Every new love interest takes on a false start.
I must gain more patience.
I can't rush this.
God's timing is not mine.
I eagerly search for a sign.
Awaiting light to be shed on this situation.
Lust's consequences aren't worth the temptation.
I trust it will be a love worth waiting for.
When God fulfills our desires, we'll want no
more.

Lead in the Light

Someday my niece and nephew will be older.

I'll miss looking over their shoulder.

I want to leave a positive legacy.

I hope they look to God for peace.

I want to thank them for being my reason:

Reason for change, growth and persevering
every season.

I want them to see me wearing the Armor of
God.

I pray that they don't go down every path I have
trod.

Little loved ones, please learn from my
mistakes.

Know your worth and raise the stakes.

Please remember your prayers.

I'm thinking of you when I can't be there.

Don't make up your mind in haste.

Remember your morals and stand on your faith.